POETIC
SCIENTIFICA
Leah Noble Davidson

This book published by University of Hell Press.
www.universityofhellpress.com

© 2013 Leah Noble Davidson

Figure 1 illustration by Phillip Stewart
www.phllpstwrt.com

Cover Art by Vince Norris
www.norrisportfolio.com

"Person" first appeared as "Harold the Zombie"
in Smalldoggies Reading Series Chapbook,
Volume 3, Summer/ Fall 2011.

Published in the United States of America.
ISBN 978-1-938753-07-7

"The experiment and the poem complete each other. The mind is made whole."

—*Jonah Lehrer*

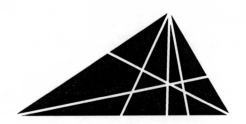

NOBODY READS
THE
INTRODUCTION

Assumptions — (1) When two individuals can closely interpret the same artifact for the same meaning, they share a language. (2) Words are artifacts of thought. (3) You and I have a tentative agreement that we think of the same thing when we see the same word (though this is rarely true— we are subject to our own internal dialects). (4) One gives meaning to a word through his culture's stories and individual experience. (5) The more experiences and stories an individual attributes to a word, the deeper its inferred meaning.

HYPOTHESIS

It is possible to give a poem deeper meaning by abstractly defining the dialect of the words of which it is composed.

Oh careful readiness, oh cinders in the jaw
you fountains of birdsong and
velvet ropes, aspiring Marilyns,

maybe, I covet you
the way you would have me do so.

Climbing into our story,
we build your image together:
a person to love, an echo
of the anecdotes strangers tell each other.
I can not hate you for being the bathtub
I drain my culture into,

for shining myself into
so many lights.

CONTENTS

63 a
64 person
66 to
67 love
68 an
69 echo

70 of
71 the
72 anecdotes
73 strangers
75 tell
76 each
77 other

78 I
79 can
80 not
81 hate
82 you
83 for
85 being
86 the
87 bathtub

88 I
89 drain
91 my
93 culture
94 into

99 for
101 shining
103 myself
104 into

106 so
107 many
109 lights

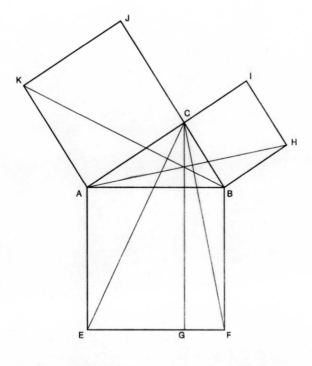

Figure (1) Proof (Euclid from Evans, 1927)

Oh

She loved out of boredom.

careful

He just wanted to fold himself into paperwork,
to date cigarette companies, wanted daytime
TV, and a little cocaine every now and then.

Death was catching. Most of us had had it for
a while, and we knew that it was just a matter of
time.

readiness

When we were 16, Chad would say that if you couldn't buy condoms with a straight face, then you shouldn't be using them.

I got my first vibrator from the 24-year-old guy I slept with the one week we broke up in high school. The guy went to Clemson. He had a boat.

The condom broke and I had to call in sick to drive up to NC for one of those day-after pills. On the way back, he stopped outside a sex shop and bought it for me. I used it for him while we drove back and a truck driver saw and honked at me. At us.

It was bright purple and looked like a rocket the Easter my dad found it and placed it in the center of my room, upright, like it was going to take off right out of the Easter basket.

A couple months later, I'd get a lesson from the crack addict I moved in with. *What you want to do is hold it 'til you almost pee your pants.*

When her toddler used to scream, she'd snatch her by the shoulders and scream right back, ask *How'd you like it.* Some nights the two of them would sit there six inches apart like smoke alarms—one head fried and the other ratted.

Back then, Chad would pull the brake going 80 on the highway. He crashed three cars in six months, and it'd take a plastic jug of pure grain to get the place quiet enough to watch a movie. Even then, you'd wake up with someone's hand down your pants, had you looking for other places pretty soon.

oh

My ex-husband found your hoodie under
my tire iron,
decided to borrow it, and it killed me
for him to know my face, the way it looks
when I almost see you; that poor man,
wearing more than he could carry,
all wrapped up in someone else's love.

cinders

The way he says goodbye is by fucking you;
it starts there.

in

I let you think "I love you" means something
because I'm trying,
the same way a mother buys and hides an
Easter basket:
I want to give you your miracle.

I know
how much you want to be in love and
you're a good man. You deserve
it, or something close, and

I'm here, not searching for
another great American soul mate. Not sure
I believe in a love like that, anymore:
a clumsy machine, nostalgic rattle in the knees
to pedestal and lean on,

a religion of endless inhale,
a dam to build in a stream of memories
for the sake of knowing
where to wash my feet in remember whens,
where to cradle matching death beds.

I don't believe in planning perfect endings
anymore,
or prayers,
but I'll say them with you.

the

When The Zombies never come, Dear,
all we'll have is time.

jaw

There was an empty gas tank where
your mouth should be,
but he found you anyway, in
the lavender and
circus legs, and
jellyfish on the streets, and,
you fool, you
unfinished masterpiece,
you folded him into your elbow

and there was a fireplace
where your mouth should be;
it was a church,
barren as Antarctica, the spiders
killed to keep warm
in the altar of your cold dead heart.

Woman, there is a boulder
where your mouth should be.
I am scratching out our language
on its surface. There is
an ugly flower
where a playground should be,
where a riot should be, a book
of broken hammers. Again and again
and again.

you

You are 8 years old and on the business end of a
gun, know already
not to throw your hands up.

You're a whore; a little stinking whore,
and you don't know what that means, but
you know that it's about waking up

without panties on, in his bed and
pretending to know what he was asking
when you didn't, and pretending not to
when you did,

and that something very grown up is
happening.

fountains

After hearing that Troy Davis' innocence was based on whether the black man wearing a yellow shirt or a white shirt killed the off-duty officer that night.

In 1989, all black men looked the same. So what does it matter: it was the cream corn one he picked. And then all that shooting happened,

and I bet he hates the moon now, on nights like that one, when it hangs in blackness like a neon canary,

and there's a reason they call it yellow journalism. But somebody killed that officer and the day shut down.

And did you know that Spanish executioners wore cheerful butter cloaks, and there were 1 2 3 4 5 other colors he could have worn that day, but what would it have mattered when all black men looked guilty.

G-i-a-l-l-o, pronounced "yellow" in Italy, refers to crime stories, both fictional and real: twenty years in prison and redacted testimonies are worth their weight in mustard gas.

And did you know in tenth-century France, they pissed that color across the doors of criminals and traitors. And did you know that in the Middle Ages, actors playing the dead highlighted themselves with it.

And did you know that when you're waiting to be executed for wearing a yellow shirt, that every night from a prison cell looks the same. I bet, the truth is,

even if he wasn't going to die, he'd hate the stench of sharp noon rising on the world like a yield sign; that frolic, that basket of gold, that frenzied lemon drizzle, that fucking happy face.

of

It was the crisp clack way her shiny red pumps made contact with the hardest surfaces that she loved the most.

birdsong

Our heartbeats are just
feathers in their mouths.

I get drunk to slow it
all down until I don't
get the poetry, either,

until I'm coughing up feathers, covered in
ventricles and thump bouquets.

and

And 13 was when I read YM
at Dawn's house and
in the back there were all these
ads for real teenage girls and
one was for a book on
How to Kiss
UPSIDE DOWN and
it was only a dollar and
I never wanted a dollar so bad
in my whole life.

velvet

I want to gather the rubies that burst from the
things you touch when you're thinking,
collect every artifact and label it *miracle,*
reverse-sighing your bus tickets, used
coffee mugs, the napkin you placed on your lap.

Every word I know becomes a shotgun.

ropes

Don't forget the yes,
shelved beside the Cheerios he ate in third grade
every day,
instead of admitting that he hated them.

It's the most important thing on the list,
better than the regret he cloisters in the cedar of
his chest—
plenty enough for the future.

A new wife. A better job. More money.
Handshakes he'll take like vitamins.
A clove of thank yous,
enough toilet paper for
the shit that will come from all of the above.

You know he needs his pain,
like sunburn you can peel for hours,
like a jar of spiders one keeps on the windowsill,
a medication for the lift-off of feet that drive you
to the store again, to needing things.

Get it wrapped for him
so he can tell I know how special it is,
a purple silk bow from aisle 6,
beside canary dish gloves and enriched potting
soil.

He can bury it in a ceramic pot (aisle 9)

and keep it in the microwave you never owned.

A camera to capture it in different kinds of light
throughout each day.
A collar to tote the microwave around in,
a hook for the collar.
a wall for the hook.

A phone for the wall. A dial tone to
contemplate.
To listen to for hours
with his new wife
and his bowl of Cheerios.

aspiring

I am failing at the careful art of silence, the weight of too many goddamn outbursts strung around my neck like an albatross.

I want to bribe my teeth into magnets so they won't open, uncage that clumsy crow that burrowed herself into the grapefruit of my tongue, making all my thank yous

sound so stupid. Last night,

I pantomimed the world's first one-woman quiet parade through your heart in celebration of the aspiring mute, a light bulb to my chest—I clicked it on and off, on and off, in an unknown Morse code, blinking out lightning bug tongues in capital letters that read, "I'M SORRY!!!" For *peeling my genuine open like a Holy Bible.* "I'M SORRY!!!" *for uncorking my enthusiasm in your general direction,* it's just that when I hear you speak, I am watching silent thought opera whistle into foghorn manifesto—

I feel like I could touch you and the air would oil, splatter like Monet canvas stretched across a vertical ocean, expand, explode like pointy house porch light on that rainy night when I was ten minutes too early, and my shy wouldn't walk me in, so my cigarette best-friended me between artificial star spark, and a door always felt like it may never open.

That half-hearted glow, it's a temporary savior:
like you, it's proof that I am not the only one
burning in the darkness with these puzzle pieces.
When I awkward into bookish, poet, cold glass
smack my lips with your notebook perfume and
kiss, and now, and fuck, and thirteenth moon,
and metaphor.

Oh metaphor, you know, it's only pretend when
you don't believe it, and I believe it. You have
changed the world, and this is me, light bulb still
stuck here, learning to love myself the way I love
your poetry.

I would drink in your inky odes until my eyes
turned coffee black and Bic-pen blue … but no
one heard a thing, especially any of you.

Marilyns

Norma knew "Marilyns" were liquid,
chirps people made to turn her toward them.
"Look at me," is all a name can say.
But it gets hot in the spotlight of a gaze,
You get to saying nothing and,
"Who does she think she is,
Marilyn Monroe?"

maybe

Your mother has Alzheimer's, so I'm preparing.
Already, you lose everything:
a box of matches,
your third pair of glasses this year,
how to spell picnicking properly.

Fifteen more years (I figure), before it kicks in
enough
to embarrass us.
So I stand behind you washing the plates,
memorizing your routines, watching your
thoughts
slip into the fog. I am collecting them:
how you spin the phone on your finger at work,
the trick to a perfect badminton serve,
why you have a scar on the meat of your chin.

I can see the future:
Your memories become orphaned scripts to
recite back to you.
The smell of lavender filling
Seattle markets in September,
her open mouth, hot against
the surface of your teeth.

Stupid with hope, I pretend to be you
sometimes to get it,
to live both our lives at once:
How to dance your half of the tango,
to hold us together.

Angry with myself, I ask questions.
I make lists. I turn off the faucet.
How to tie a shoelace.
Where home is.

Only the most diligent moments remain
stained in the muscles of your face—
the wrinkles in your eyes are twenty years of
programming,
a pit beneath your cheek: all your best
comebacks.
The rest will wash away:
how we first met, my name.

We lose everything.

I

A professor told me not to use *that letter*
as the subject of a poem.

I don't remember her name.

covet

I thought we were robots, so I turned your
mouth into a nest of wires, and then you said
I love you perfectly.

You said it over and over again, except,
every time the moon came out: bees.

you

All wrapped up in the air
like a sexy human burrito.

the

The bridesmaids on Tenth and Galleria
are drunk—
fell off their high heels, unchased.

way

After Jamaica Kincaid's "Girl"

She loved you, Jamaica. Your mother
knew to respect you enough to
be the thorns in your side when

the world is an angry hole. She knew
to make you hard, to make you hate
her splitting tongue, to teach

you about sweeping the corner, and
men. She knew you had
a spirit in you and couldn't let you

grow
without someone
to prove wrong.

you

You are 8 years old and on the hateful end of a gun.

(1) This has happened before.

(2) This will happen again.

(3) You will learn not to throw your hands up

(4) like a victim.

(5) She dies.
In the same kitchen where she calls you
a whore
for being younger so much younger
for drawing her husband in like that.

(6) It will happen again. All of it,
the kitchen and the death.

(7) You will learn that shame is a tool
for the desperate
who believe in the safety of locked doors.

(8) You will lock your door
and hope
and hope for nothing.

(9) You will learn the science behind triggers
and forgive them.

You forgive all of them.

would

I was so alone that summer,
that first day the sun pushed
electric chalk clouds
across that bruised ceiling
and stayed there

shoulders ripened, breasts swelled,
everyone looked familiar, walked on
the same side of the street. I had never seen
so many party teeth atop bicycles,

arms flailed and helicoptered over
peony dresses. Everything orange
popped. Everything pregnant popped.

Tongues grew long in want
to taste new things:
couples fell from the sky
flapping their grandiose intention wings
like naked skydivers magnetized by
something they weren't sick of yet.

I could smell the grass sprinting. The
sepia of dusk made my eyes water.
I didn't care what time I got there;
I would go.

have

The depression begins with you fingering hand towels you can't afford in a store you'll never remember the name of because you're consumed with how they remind you of the ones you dried the dishes with when you quit working to stay home with the baby while he started his career at the job that you got for him so he wouldn't have to work nights at the bookstore, pretended to be him, wrote the résumé and answered the emails. You researched how to ace an interview, picked out and ironed his clothes.

He could buy you these towels if you hadn't left because he threw you across the kitchen floor, told you how much you owed him, but that money is for flowers now, for a woman much prettier than you, someone he's learned to be thankful for.

me

I love to watch a woman cry
when it's not my fault,

all whale eyes and train stop,
the wipe and fuck of it,
the wind and explanation.

The way she unfolds
from the tear ducts, vibrates
from cherry gloss to stiletto,

mascara racing,
a precious humanity welling up in her
shoulders,
ancient and wordless.

I couldn't squash a ballet like that with a tissue,
wouldn't distract her to say, "Thanks."

do

Dear John,

You are avocado in a woman's hands,
the ugliness you readily embrace
barely thick enough to call skin,

you are beautiful,
love being peeled by her fingers,
love how she drops your angry jaw to the floor,

how she still thinks she can make something
of you
when you are the comfort meat
she doesn't know will change her

will travel thousands of miles
to land at her dinner plate whole,
split yourself into pieces willingly,
draw across her tongue.

Let her swallow you, John,
if only to keep her alive
one more day.

SO

(1) So, it's 1955 and Superman is in a pickle, flipping through the phonebook under "S": "Service," "Seamstress," and he finds a list of names: Barbara, Betty, Carol, Susanne. "Susanne," he says with a finger plop, goes for the phone but stops short. This is the third day he's started this way since he decided that having your mom measure your super suit—*having your mom measure your junk*—that's just not going to cut it anymore. But how does a man explain the need for a spandex suit and cape? "It's not enough that I can fly—I want to be a hero and there's no glory in vanilla: wrap me in saffron and rubies, Susanne. Wrap me in saffron and rubies."

(2) My little bean is almost 6, and like me, he wants to do everything. Dog-eared leap and thunderclap under feet, he is trying to fly. He's got imaginary engines strapped to his ankles, cloud ground a lottery ticket away and I say, "Go for it," because he's made of magic—he can heal his own splintered bones, but I can't bandage a broken spirit, and I know that one day he's going to forget to remember to forget about the gravity of a thing. I want to tell him that nothing will ever feel more real than the first time you imagine it. And, baby, you have already conquered flight:

49

Remember that time we colored paper wings and flew to Neptune for a picnic (and it looked just like our backyard)? Watched ice rocks connect star dots before burning through the atmosphere. You called to me, "Mommy, that one over there! See its burst and fade?"

(3) Swan dive from 20 stories high and tell me if the glory is in the landing or the leap.

(4) The only difference between a bungee drop and a toddler hop is perspective.

(5) My childhood was a firefly in a summer breeze, except, instead of a firefly, it was an empty suitcase, and instead of a summer breeze, it was a falling plane. My favorite lovers were always trying to save me, as if, one day, I would eggshell shatter. As if, one day, I would land.

(6) When you step onto the plane, look down and smile at your shoes for me, for they hold your feet, which have brought you thus far. Like me, your shoes will never doubt you; they will simply follow your direction, and thus, can take you anywhere you want to go. How lucky they are to travel with you in your silence and your folly.

(7) Gravity is a direct result of the earth's mass drawing us in. For every force that pulls something to the ground, there is another force pulling it away: we are not quite as stuck to the world as we think we are; we are merely always falling, giving in to the weight of it.

Climbing

The sky tossed 1.3 billion tiny ping pong balls
to the ground in rally.

Frozen spheres smashed windows
two at a time.

Every game built on itself
until it became impossible to tell
the score.

Cars stopped.

Grown men
surfaced tables with picket fence grins
and children scrambled for nets.

Sunset red smacked black top,
chopped faults along the crevices of buildings,
shook hands with the night shift lights,
and spun itself into tomorrow.

Someone tried to tell us that
it was all hail—something about
air pressure looping
the balls along the backhand push of the storm,

but we knew better,
gripping our paddles
and counting to eleven.

into

I never yelled.

I'd sworn that if it ever happened again
that the man would not survive,
that I would die before—

but I only asked that he not go inside of me,

and when he let his mess
cling to my belly, my ripped panties,
not only did he survive,

but I thanked him.

our

Before pretty Marilyn in blonde nudes
with painted cheeks for *Time* or Sinatra,

normal Norma stood alone and perfect
behind clumsy glasses and a smile.

I wonder if Joe ever knew her.

story

You die and everyone finds out before me because we are almost strangers—except that you and that guy I used to date fell in love.

And outside, the socialites are everyone and everyone is crying while I become best friends with your ghost and that's when I know it's a dream.

And the night I tell you about it, we fuck like optometrists drink—you and me and my new and old boyfriend, which is also a dream,

and the part where the old one and I get tired, put on our clothes and smoke at the window while you finish,

"He's not bad," the old one says.

You are gorgeous. I say nothing in a nod and half a swallow.

we

I love (leaving) you because I know
how far you'll go to keep me.

build

How "Falling in Love" is like moving into a new home: It sucks to do alone.

For those of us who do it in pairs, one person usually has more junk than the other, and when both people have a lot of junk, you need the help of some good friends.

You are usually more excited about these moves than your friends are, who are hoping that this will be the last time they have to help you move your heavy shit from one place to another.

Good thing, love goes well with pizza and beer.

When you are in love, it always seems like it's someone else's at first. At first, you never know where to put your stuff, is this the bedroom or the kitchen? Do we do our laundry here, or entertain ourselves?

And then, new undiscovered corners of the house seem fun and interesting, even if they were things you used to hate about other people's houses. Or even your last house—sometimes, you'll find that you have only moved into a different version of the place that you just left, and no matter how hard you try to make it work,

Some places, you'll find, they aren't for you,

or your roommate,who decides to move on, because they had unrealistic expectations of the house, or hated yard work, or couldn't stop seeing themselves in the houses down the street; regardless, you may then find yourself trying to convince someone new to move into this home you just can't leave.

Such people are the same type to travel great distances to peer into their old windows, expecting everything to be the same except no one really lives there anymore.

I do not recommend this type of behavior.

Even if it leaves you destitute and homeless: in all probability, you will find somewhere to be and, if you're lucky, may you stumble into your perfect home unplanned, whether it's one you hardly see, but love all the same, or one you learn to know in a constant comfortable way, a place to grow old in, with just enough sun on the front door, walls to write your name on, attics to bundle up nostalgic baubles ....

You'll learn to dance on the floors in your socks; find a hiding cellar. You'll spend just the right amount of time tidying up, washing the windows, sweeping out the closets, rearranging the furniture.

The process slows, but you never really stop moving in. At night, old familiar sounds will comfort even the most worn places.

your

Now that you are gone, our language
is dead, does not rattle between
two coffee cups.

It sits in the air, waiting.

image

Your expression is so proud.

It is one hour until it is not your birthday anymore
and you are looking deep into every eye to make
sure we are all sincere
until you have had enough to drink.

You have been doing this all night.

You are sliding your hand up my thigh
in the kitchen, whisking me away to
the anonymous open
of the living room to kiss me
where no one will see
because they are all
looking at themselves in the black mirrors
windows make for the desperate awake.

Your smile is easy, but the wrinkle in your brow
that you unlock for me—
that look reminds me that I am less sorry
for ignoring you those first few months
than for all the nicest things I ever said to you.

You were right. I could never tell the future—
only see potential, split the foolish from the
thieves.

You know which one you are.
Happy Birthday.

together

We were admired by only each other.

a

A is for Anna, the woman you will fall in love with next year, who wraps her opus in alabaster eyes; Anna's hello echo will crush your throat like a trash compactor. And b. B is for the second word you'll think you have for a sight like Anna walking by, but, to fold a smoke like that on to paper, you've got to have c and d words.

person

Harold the Zombie is picking his wounds again—
the moon must feel as gray and distant.
Jennifer asks him if he feels like
a pitted olive cheese. "No,
only brains."

Harold wants to be a vegan, wants
to quit smoking, and learn Pilates. He wants to
watch less TV, but it keeps him off the streets,
out of people's heads,
out of his own head,

keeps him from thinking about
his abandoned strawberry heart
all rotted in a Safeway bag
still hugging the curb of an L.A. street, and
inching with the wind between
highway static and beautiful buildings that broil
in Artemis poses.

Harold keeps his keys in the space
where his heart is gone,

and he likes the china clang they make
in his chest when he sings to his dead heart.
On those days, his head
is a pop song, and his body is a boom box.
On those days, he curls his heels in broken
strides that shuffle unnatural but loving beats;

Harold wants to buy that poor heart some
Mylar balloons and candles.
He wants it to know that he's coming back for it
someday.

Jennifer holds her hand over that hole when
he makes love to her, holding the keys
in the place where his heart used to be,
watches them shine like a trophy.

Sometimes she gets out her thread and webs
his keys in place like a San Francisco
earthquake system.

There are no self-help books for
falling in love with the dead
so the two of them stay up all night
peeling over Harold's losses:

Jennifer is buying Velcro;
Harold is learning French—

he loves telling her romantic-sounding
things she can't understand.
In French, he confesses, I used
the last of the toilet paper.
"Nous sont faibles sur le papier hygiénique."
In French, he confesses, Sometimes
I fantasize about your mother's brains.
"Parfois je fantasize de votre mère du cerveau."

He confesses, "S'il vous plaît, de mon amour,
permettez-moi en outre automne."
Please, my love, let me fall apart.

to

"You do not have to be good."
                    —From *Wild Geese* by **Mary Oliver**

He said that maybe Mary would be different
if God had been polite,
had asked her before
fucking her
as so many men are used to doing,

and so our story goes
to men grabbing and calling
and we are to be great statues
for them,
unbeatable,
naming ourselves in spite of,
because of our goodness, our
unnecessary kindnesses,

taking on thrones, our throats
great caverns of holiness
to fight after—what a great story, this
"woman" one. I tell you,

I want a man that doesn't need to ask
but does. He doesn't have to be
good.

love

Christmas is coming; she's
lacing the streets with a darkness
wrapped in lights, store windows
wagging their tongues at
every couple that's
trying to make it to February.

an

"Too Good For This" is shopping for a date at the poetry reading; "The Show I Did Not Come To See" squeezes behind, between, and in front of me, to shuffle and lean, bend my neck like a listening dog.

This warehouse, a closet of daydreamers, recycling mistakes into heavy diaphragms, and all I can do is notice her knees hugging negative space,

how "Aren't You Something" has found herself in unfamiliar waters of sweet talk and side smiles.

"Thinks She Invented A Weapon" wrapped her ass in white flags, has an infant fruit stilted on two spindly branches, and she's not going to smile at me:

I have never been young, never called to the snakes like an open wound.

echo

I stopped counting days
when your eyes went photocopy,

forgot that we were ever everyday
that we were *see you in two hours*
I can't wait for your lips
and your fingers felt like *fingers,*

dance me into film noir beach
losing shoes in bioluminescent graffiti and mean it:
really really far away and back again.

Your love letters were so stunning
the way you never wrote them,

too many to remember the way we were
before the flat black empty .
before the flat black empty .
before the flat black empty .
before the flat black empty .

of

I open the love letter and a tiny ninja jumps out
to join the others: the cowboy, the poet, the bear.

They are all fighting on my coffee table
as if they are real.

the

The day you left, I called in
sick to work and masturbated
all day in silence

until it was easy to think of you
as a lovely tool, until
I could touch myself and feel nothing.

anecdotes

I liked his girlfriend who
would later dump him over
a condom wrapper
he left on the floor for three weeks.
She saw it, and there was an awkward ride
to the beach, "Tell me who you're fucking,"
she demanded, and wouldn't believe
that he was just messy. So he
moved to Budapest to cool off.
Funny thing about that—
he had this one poem about that girl
where he compared her to
the moon and an old house and
I wanted to be his wobbly table
every time I read it,
seemed like he really loved her,
he had a way with words
and a thing for one quiet girl.
I bet he picks up more often, now.

strangers

After seven years together, he turns to me and says, "When we met, you said you'd make my life more interesting—I guess you kind of dropped the ball on that one." So I pack my clothes into a basket, and I leave him. Just like that.

I tell him he can have everything else.

"Keep the house we made a home, the walls we painted, the pictures we took and hung, and the kitchen table on which I kicked your ass at chess, and scrabble, and rummy.

Keep the garden in the back, the raspberries along the fence, and the sauces I made in the cupboard.

Keep the dishes I washed lovingly after Sunday breakfasts and homemade dinners. Keep the 1200-dollar, 200-pound, 1945 Steelcase Airstream desk I found in perfect condition for free, and snuck into the house without your knowing for a week.

Keep the books we used to read aloud together, taking turns at night and waiting for a tap to peel the page in case the other was asleep. Keep the walking sticks we made along the Appalachian Trail, the bracelet from when I thought going to Juárez would be a good idea and we almost died.

Keep the car in which we drove to Savannah on a whim, we fought in in San Francisco, the one we slept in in the Redwood Forest after you left our tent stakes on a beach in Malibu (I remember what a dream that seemed like).

Keep the clothes I mended for you, the buttons I sewed on last-minute before your interviews. Keep the bed on which we conceived our son, keep the poems I wrote while you were sleeping beside him after he was born, keep the blanket he carried for his first two years and the pictures I took of him last week at the park. You can have it all, and I will keep what is left of my dignity.

I've lost that flame for you, I am burned at both ends, and the broken parts you thought you fixed were only hiding between my rib bones, while I waited for you to fall in love, to forgive me for my folly, lust, and spontaneity.

I have folded myself into you, but I have grown tired of your inertia, of playing your entertainer and failing over and over and over."

I tell him, "I have always been good at saying goodbye, bowing out before the screaming, and the tears, and the heavy on my knees. You have taught me well, Love, how to feel these things alone. I can't share these things with you.

Good luck, though, finding someone who'll keep your interest."

tell

So you are in a boat without language and I have a stick for a mouth. You are you and I'm waving the stick like it means something and you start jumping up and down. So, now the boat is rocking and my stick, it topples over, and you have an idea.

You throw everything into the water. Now, we have nothing in a boat without language—only a set of grasps to share, the side of a hull, a wooden seat. And you can't ask me what I think of gravity and I can't say it's bunk, and you can't think, "I disagree," because there are no words in your head.

Just a picture, a moving picture of what we won't call water and a loss for something not a stick.

each

I think it was when I told you that I wanted
to see your brain scattered like sugar glass
screeching primitive rainbows across the floor

that I became ridiculous or rude or creepy
with all my dangerous bubblegum spit corrupting
your dignified stand on Ginsberg.

Maybe I was being melodramatic, but
it was such a handsome day, and I didn't want
to stub it on affordable debate;

it's just that I was scavenger hunting for freckles
and you were cleaning the bathroom.

other

See Echo.
See Fountains,
see Image, Into,
Maybe.
See Marilyns.
See Ropes.
See Story.
See Strangers.
See Tell. See Would.
See You.

I

If you are the subject
of your own art, it is easy

to mistake your art's value
for your own.

can

Twice a month,
my roommate holds
an eight-lady dinner party.

He likes cooking for
beautiful women
he can't have.

Spinach
Cheese
Onions
Mushrooms
Fruit, for the salad
yes, that's all he needs.

not

I never told my mom that he asked and I said
yes (/let us down),
I would never tell my son or a crowd—
these shapes enough, mute gates.

The monster was a teenage boy, Tesla, maybe,
started cigarettes, visiting my bunk.
There was not enough room,
and it hurt because I was so little (see,
I do it again here—a push when
no one's looking yet, an undirected gasp).

Ask me straight, and nothing happened.

I am picking up my boy and his new pop-up art
from school and he puts it to his face.

I am writing; he is asking questions.
He could be a balloon. He says, "Look Mom,
I could be a monster."

hate

And he says,
"They hate me."

And I say,
"They hate the way your fear
makes them feel."

And I say,
"Baby, hand them a smile
made for who they want to be, and they'll smile
back like that."

you

There's a grown man howling in my rental car
because you wouldn't smile at him. I can't
hate you for that.

for

Everyone knows you're the victim.
No one thinks you started the fight:

when I was younger, and my earthquakes
were too much for me to handle, I would ~~beg~~
dare him into throwing punches,

but he was never man enough to hit me,
so I'd hurl my twiggy fists into
the garbage disposal looking for
poetry in the way a man will
avalanche to his knees and plead,

the way he will mop the floors with
the flood of his backbone, and fault his lips
to survive a woman who knows

affection is the momentum of a budded fist
plowing fractured blooms into her body.

It takes a strong man not to
stoke that fire, let her burn herself alive,
watch her wade through cinders,
praying to an altar of crude oil,

for him to forage the forest of his heart
for picket fence dreams and
stack them at her feet soaked in kerosene—

he will always be stuck in her aftershock.
Not all women with a history of shiny

garbage bag eyes know to speak victim,
finding shelter in the loss of a softness
unaffordable.

Some of us learn to wrap our hearts
in newspaper
and fold men like matchbooks.

being

Dearest Phoenix, if you are empty with
running anthems to your own funeral,
know that I am done fuming, have been
accruing Los Angeles in my closet
for your broken February, when
peony skirts blacken to umbrellas.
I guess I'm just waiting for you to die already
so that we can get on with the fireworks.

the

Before she warms up to her own empty arms,
remember you're playing the long game.

bathtub

My mother taught me how to prepare for
That kind of misery:

I would feel it coming on, knew to
go to the store and buy
vegetables and juices and crackers.

I could get there and back in time to
get to the tub, crawl inside
and rock in the water.

I

My God! You're right! I'm a martyr.

drain

Sleeplessness spreads her long legs into
the blank spaces of your apartment,
aches her back into your ceiling, dazzles the fan.

She remembers
how to tuck herself into
the paper nests of your ears, whispers
in old blue alligator tongue,
says nothing. Hers

is the language of the space between.

It would be wrong to assume she speaks
summer lake.

She knows pillow talk:
threads her purple hair into
your favorite sheets,
pulls your teeth from her stomach

and lines them along your kitchen sink
according to scientific name:

one is an ankle stretching for the cab last
Thursday,
one is an expensive thirsty dog,
a fur coat,
a megaphone,
a siren,

a siren of salty teeth stacked along your dirty sink,
and you, you pillbox, you keep thanking her—
that stare!

What do you expect from all this cowered
whittling?
A windfall, perhaps? A blanket of expectations?
A marriage of rooms within rooms? A plastic
door to ask her into?

my

After he stained hand-shaped bruises
around my mother's throat,
dad could not understand
why she drove the plains between us.
> *Line-dried sheets in Kansas*
> *are wilted angels swaying in*
> *tomato blossom and nostalgia.*

Grandma always hated how
I'd run through them with my dirty hands.

He got four rounds off once, trying to prove
how right she was, before they pulled
the barrel from his hands—long and hot as my
mother's neck.
> *Remember that the anvil was birthed*
> *beneath hammers. It is heavy, rock-like*
> *for good reason, remember*
> *how it sings for the one who beats it.*

Sometimes I wake up washing laundry; it's
easy. It is so easy to grow up tortured by
horrifying people. What is hard is
forgiving yourself for being no different.

It is the heaviest thing in the world to
carry the pain of all the people who have hurt
because they loved you,

to stain the corners of your mouth with
them, to hide them there, and try to lift them
every time you smile.

He had the most beautiful hands
on the only day I remember him sober,
when he wilted at my frailty.
The sheets behind him
were a perfect shade of white.

culture

You can smell it from the parking lot,

before the seagull squawks
and the bikini girls laid out in sweaty buffets
of burning meat season the air,
as memorable as your nana's chicken stock:

that fragrant comfort seeps
into your blood,

the way pavement holds the rain
and offers it back to sandaled feet,

the way melting snow can
drift through a bus
packed to the emergency lights
with damp handmade mittens and unwashed
T-shirts.

into

I have always had this thing against hallways, which exist solely as corridors between here and there: when you are in a hallway, you are never really anywhere—space and time cannot pill themselves into the tiny throats of hallways, and anything is possible.

(Age 20) I am at six doors towing parallel lines like soldiers ready to fight, and the lady on the phone says Josh died honorably. I just wanted him to be Superman.

Smaller. (Age 6) When she couldn't handle the way I stapled her down, my mother would send me off to anyone willing to help. Each new house felt like sandpaper soap, and I shrank my body into corner smiles—I could be 4 or 5 for you, if you wanted dandelion braids for rent.

The hallways flaunted picture frames that would never miss me, full of the people ready to show their teeth—I always hoped for dishwasher over sex doll.

Bigger. (8) Casey says if I ever tell my mom what he did, that he'll hang me upside down in the hallway and beat me with a baseball bat. He is not lying.

Bigger. (16) My boyfriend gets home strip club

drunk. Angry. When I won't fuck him his fist burst through wall like sugar.

Bigger. (19) Jordan borrows Chad's keys to unlock my front door; I'm in the hall when he shows me how a real man doesn't need to ask for permission.

Smaller. (Age 13) I am sleeping outside mom's locked bedroom door while she fucks her man because this is as close as I can get to her affection. It was always my favorite place to do the cutting.

Smaller. (11) My mom and him laugh when he tells her that I couldn't stop crying after he threw me down the hall. *You really shoulda seen her face in midair.*

Smaller. (Age 4) I'm sitting on the step between the kitchen and the living room of my mother's first trailer while she watches *Nightmare on Elm Street*, and I have to pee. To my right, cackles epileptic-inducing color/black/ color/black—to my left, a mine field of linoleum, and an empty velvet hole in the wall filled with razor fingers and angry teeth. Even then, I knew the choice was embarrassment or certain death. I knew what to do.

(28) I am learning to stop renting apartments with hallways. They bring out the monsters in people.

for

*She threw her two children off the Sellwood Bridge
that morning. Threw* falls from teeth like wooden
blocks—as if her own blood would fight her.
Threw. As if she couldn't drop her babies
softly.

I picture the powder blue light of rush hour
peeling down from its edges,
the breath of night breaking early on their necks,

not the eyes,
but the muscles around them, that mean
more about confusion than fear.

the hands gripping at air,

> little
> gasping
> starfish.

A pink shoelace in free fall.

The little girl survived by holding on to
her toddler brother's dead body. It's horrible.

Listen, I drove to the bridge, her bridge
its stone is not as cold as I had thought—
her last *I love yous* hang in the air. It's beautiful.
The water is still a giant rolling
firework, a magic blanket for goodbye,

still a gentle heaven.

They must have been heavy,
I told the echo, did not try to
bring it back. We were
so quiet together.

There was nothing to say.

shining

He slips into me with all the casualness
of a gas station attendant making
change, a drug dealer weighing out a dime bag,
a single mother popping aspirin.

The currency of this has no gold standard.

I know brains, how they
thrive on making connections,
neurons jumping strawberry meat caverns, how
the same parts you use to make a memory are
the parts you use to make a decision,

how compassion is chemical,
"love," that thing we consider saying when
the novelty drug starts wearing off.

I am looking for his weaknesses like an architect
deconstructs a building, skinning his actions
down to living bone.

There are no fault lines.

We are made up of the people who survived—
or the ones that didn't die before procreating.
Millions of years and this is what we are:
weak-less.

There were nights when our sex danced on the
ceiling,

before he told me how much he loved me
and his eyes became bricks,
hollow windows, drywall, strawberries.

myself

with the seriousness
only capable of a 4-year-old

into

My grandmother smeared her guts on canvas for
money, could draw your gawk with pencil, and
sketch anything real with the right medium. I am
the granddaughter of two painters.

An artist, she magnified emotion into odes,
turned con men into lovers.

My grandmother abandoned a good man for the
con artist who left her
and she heard more men calling, death dogs
in gentlemen's shoes circling dangling legs of her
children at the table.

A woman, she was genetically
wired to forgive pain,

gentlemen's shoes, hourglass teeth exposed, ghost
of a home fading to white, pupilless eyes of moving
bodies, little fingers, snow storms, laughing
cheeks of cotton,
grass-bladed hair gone empty.

Shot herself in the head while her children were
home.

Snatched her own life with a click, the click
nothing more than the lock of a hammer,
ingenuity of man, stomp of a thumb,
that could be practiced out of its sacred

sound, until she couldn't hear

what it represented.

Suicide is a con. I imagine heels across a kitchen
floor, or crickets calling out to the dusk, until
her trigger finger couldn't feel it anymore:

Classically trained, she knew how careful
practice of art
produces a perfect finish.

SO

You are in a boat in a lake where you can see the bottom of the lake and I am at the bottom of the lake with a picture that I want you to see,

and I'm moving the picture around for you. And you, in the boat, wade through gallons of meaning, like reconstructing spiderwebs with superglue.

There is nothing I can do to make you see the picture.

There's so much distance.

many

Like when they dig
me into the sod or peat moss
or organic filler material
or they scatter me

and I am not some
sad memory, just away,
like the friend who leaves
for a better job,
or more like childhood,

like that, when I am
more grounded than I was
in motion—
especially in thought
or long embrace

with fists that will not
close again
and a choir of glamour shots
float up into lowered
conversations
over cheap wine
and sliced salami,

and maybe a few tear up
over an American Spirit outside
on a day with
too much swagger,

and the air
fills with a need to
do more than stand like this
and remember:

this is how I know your quietness,
a shroud of wishes
twisted around
surrender,

as if an organ were
playing the saddest
swing song
in your refrigerator,

and someone, now,
was contemplating a tattoo
of what you'd say
if you could.

Once, we broke a window, and
remember how
no one noticed
like we thought they would?

The glass let go easily
into a billion tiny chimes
like confetti,
like new beginnings
or different kinds of deaths.

lights

The surfaces of seas and lakes often
reflect skylight,
enhancing the inherent blue of water:
the deeper the pool, the bluer the water. You
were always so deep.

I'm sorry I called you watercolor,
and what I meant was I can't hear you yet,
what I meant was take me with you,
and you heard, *Get it together, kid.*
Find the lines.

Rain is actually blue.

Sometimes, though, we're just too close to
see it, like that night the drunk wore off and I
watched your face age, your
genu-hopeful swing seat rise and fall from me
like a hand plane, oil drill, stop-short inhale.

Rainfall is measured through
the use of rain gauges. They found no such
gauges in Egypt, where the oldest existing
paintings are watercolors.

They were there for years before someone
stumbled
over them—deep, heavy, and full of
words. Because watercolor is translucent,
genuine,

because it reflects light back to its audience,
painting over flaws becomes impossible.

Its strength is in the way it fakes weight
in weightlessness like rain. Like us:
imaginary hand grenades, amplified feathers.

Rain is liquid precipitation, which, unlike snow,
sleet, or hail, drops Kandinsky, Schiele, Cézanne,
stunning like you.

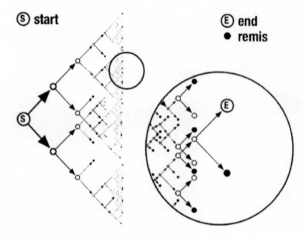

Figure (2) Structural diagram of branching narrative.
The possible courses of a game of chess with iu multilinear
ramifications far exceed anything an interactive narrative
scaffold could support -- the only clearly defined structural
attributes are the beginning and end of the game (Wand,
2011).

References

Evans, George W. (1927). "Postulates and Sequence in Euclid." The Mathematics Teacher, 20, 310-20.

Wand, E. (2002). Interactive Storytelling: The Renaissance of Narration in New Screen Media- Cinema/Art/Narrative, M. Rieser and A. Zapp (eds.), British Film Institute, London.

This observational poetic record was inspired by a combination of language studies, behavioral and cognitive psychology, and visual culture. Author would like to thank John Survivor Blake, Tyler Atwood, Johnny No Bueno, Brian S. Ellis, Robyn Bateman, Eirean Bradley, IWPS, Derrick Brown, Mindy Nettifee, Gerowe Simmons, Backspace, Landon and Porter Davidson, Carrie Seitzinger and Matty Byloos, Kim Noble, the Portland Poetry Slam, Michael Francis Rizzo, 74, Mike McGee, Randy Darris, Doc Luben, Dwayne King, Phillip Stewart, and the Portland Metro Area Transit.

Leah Noble Davidson has a curious 6-year-old and the charismatic precision of a spy. She lives in Portland, OR. This is her first book of poetry.

Available from University of Hell Press:

by Eirean Bradley
the I in team

by Calvero
someday i'm going to marry Katy Perry

by Leah Noble Davidson
Poetic Scientifica

by Brian S. Ellis
American Dust Revisited

by Greg Gerding
The Burning Album of Lame
Venue Voyeurisms: Bars of San Diego
Loser Makes Good: Selected Poems 1994
Piss Artist: Selected Poems 1995-1999
The Idiot Parade: Selected Poems 2000-2005

by Lindsey Kugler
HERE.

by Johnny No Bueno
We Were Warriors

by Stephen M. Park
High & Dry

UNIVERSITY OF HELL PRESS

universityofhellpress.com

CPSIA information can be obtained at www.ICGtesting.com
Printed in the USA
BVOW08s1301270813

329556BV00001B/2/P